THE PERSONALISM
OF JOHN PAUL II

THE PERSONALISM
OF JOHN PAUL II

JOHN F. CROSBY

HILDEBRAND

PROJECT

The essays in this book originally appeared in the magazine *Lay Witness* in
2000.
The appendix was originally commissioned by The Personalist Project,
and appears on their website: www.thepersonalistproject.org.
We gratefully acknowledge both organizations for their permission to
publish the works, with minor edits, in this new edition.

Published 2019 by Hildebrand Press
1235 University Blvd., Steubenville, Ohio 43952

Publisher's Cataloging-in-Publication Data
Crosby, John F., 1944–, author.
The Personalism of John Paul II / by John F. Crosby.
Steubenville, OH: Hildebrand Press, 2019.

ISBN 978-1-939773-14-2
LCCN 2019933579

Subjects: LCSH John Paul II, Pope, 1920–2005. | Personalism. | Ethics. |
Christian ethics—Catholic authors. | Phenomenology. | Religion—
Philosophy. | BISAC RELIGION / Christianity /
Catholic | PHILOSOPHY / Individual Philosophers | PHILOSOPHY /
Movements / Phenomenology
Classification: LCC BX1378.5 .C76 2019 | DDC 230/.2/0924—dc23

Typeset by Kachergis Book Design
Set in Monotype Perpetua, a typeface designed by English sculptor Eric Gill

Front Cover Font: Hoefler Text
Cover Image: *St Peter's and the Vatican from the Gardens of the Villa
Barberini, Rome*, by J.M.W. Turner, part of *Rome: Colour Studies
Sketchbook* at the Tate
Image Source: Licensed from Tate Images

Production and cover design by Christopher T. Haley

www.hildebrandproject.org

For my dear wife, Pia.

CONTENTS

PREFACE

I wrote this little book twenty years ago as an intro-
duction to the main themes in St. John Paul II's personalism. I reissue it today in the conviction that his
personalism is needed now no less than it was then.
Many are the depersonalizing forces that beset us today. We continue to see in our time what St. John
Paul called the "pulverization of the person." And
yet, at the same time, we continue to see signs of a
growing personalist sensibility. Deep down most of
us know that persons merit respect and should not
be manipulated and commodified and demonized.
Even when we are complicit in some such abuse of
persons, we know better. Our better self revives
when we are rebuked. And so we need to fan the
flames of a certain sense for the person that has not
been extinguished in the men and women of our

time. We need to hear a prophetic voice that calls us back to the "truth about man" that is still felt in our conscience. John Paul II is just the voice we need to hear.

John F. Crosby

January 26, 2019

Steubenville, OH

THE PERSONALISM
OF JOHN PAUL II

Chapter One

"FLYING WITH BOTH WINGS": WHY CHRISTIANS NEED PHILOSOPHY

We don't have to listen to Pope John Paul II for long before noticing his fascination with the human person. We are struck by how often and how passionately he speaks about the dignity of the person. He has become a kind of prophet of personal dignity, witnessing to it before the conscience of mankind like no other world leader, indeed, like no previous pope. In fact, this affirmation of the person is perhaps the central theme of all his thought and teaching. We can't begin to understand him if we do not understand this personalist passion of John Paul.

Now when he speaks about the person, he of course announces the faith of the Church, the faith entrusted to the apostles. He speaks about the dignity that persons have as images of God, as brothers and sisters of the God-man, Jesus Christ. He can't quote often enough the text from Vatican II that says that Christ reveals man to man himself. But if we listen closely, we will find that he speaks not only from the point of view of faith—there is something more in his teaching. What is it?

Let us look at the striking opening line of Pope John Paul II's 1998 encyclical, *Fides et Ratio*: "Faith and reason are like two wings on which the human spirit rises to the contemplation of truth." Notice: not faith alone, but faith *and* reason. It is not Catholic to say we want only faith and we leave reason to the pagans; the Catholic way is faith and reason. And by reason the encyclical means *philosophical* reason. Pope John Paul II is not speaking of reason as exercised by the natural sciences such as biology or chemistry; he is not saying that faith and natural science are two wings on which the human spirit rises to the contemplation of truth. Though he has shown throughout his pontificate great esteem for the natural sciences, they do not represent one of

the two wings. Rather, he means that it is faith
and philosophical reason that are like two wings
on which the human spirit rises to the contemplation of truth.

It follows from the logic of this metaphor that
faith is bound to suffer when philosophical reason
is neglected. The believer is then like a bird trying to fly with only one wing. Thus we read in
Fides et Ratio: "[D]eprived of reason, faith has stressed
feeling and experience, and so runs the risk of no
longer being a universal proposition." He says in another place in the encyclical that the Church cannot
even articulate her faith without employing the
resources of philosophy. In addition, he stresses
the importance of philosophy for evangelizing the
nations. For when we Catholics address nonbelievers, we cannot begin by quoting the Bible
and the magisterial teaching of the Church; we
rather begin by first seeking out common ground
with them by means of philosophical reason,
which nonbelievers share with believers. It is on
just this common ground of reason that Pope John
Paul II stands when, for example, he addresses
the General Assembly of the United Nations.

Here, then, is the other thing that we can detect in Pope John Paul II's proclamation of the truth about the human person: Besides announcing the faith of the Church, he also uses philosophical reason to understand the person more deeply and to explain the truth about the person more convincingly. He has developed an entire personalist philosophy and constantly employs it in his addresses and writings.

The purpose of this book is to introduce the reader to the personalist philosophy of Pope John Paul II. By reading the chapters that follow, you will be able to find more in the Holy Father's teachings the next time you read them, and thus you will understand him more deeply. You may also enrich your own faith by learning to fly with the wings of both faith and reason.

Pope John Paul II thinks that it is especially important at the beginning of the 21st century to give attention to philosophy, including the philosophy of the person. In *Fides et Ratio*, he acknowledges that philosophy has fallen on hard times. Many philosophers no longer believe in philosophy; they deny that philosophy can establish any firm result; they deny that it can contribute to our understanding of the meaning of existence. They have, in effect, despaired of philosophy.

Even you and I are much more affected by this loss of confidence in philosophical reason than we realize. For example, when we talk about the human embryo, we tend to think that our one source of knowledge about embryos is biology, or the branch of it called embryology. We think if we go beyond embryology in our understanding of the embryo and affirm that the embryo is a person with rights, *then we do so by means of faith*. In other words, we tend to think that the two sources for our understanding of the embryo are science and faith. We entirely overlook philosophy and all that we can understand about the human embryo by means of philosophical reason.

And so, the Holy Father sees it as one of his most important pastoral tasks to exhort philosophers to dare to do philosophy again. It is an unusual position for a pope to be in. At the end of the nineteenth century, Pope Leo XIII had to resist the arrogance of reason and defend the faith of the Church against rationalistic intrusions. But at the end of the twentieth century Pope John Paul II had to defend reason against unreason. He knows how much faith needs reason, and so he cannot remain indifferent to a situation in which people have lost confidence in reason.

What concerns us in this book is that we Christians can't do justice to the human person without restoring philosophy to its proper place and letting it collaborate with faith more than we are used to doing.

Pope John Paul II is ideally suited to lead us into the philosophy of the person. He is a philosopher-pope like no previous successor of St. Peter. Besides the usual seminary studies in philosophy, Pope John Paul II went much deeper into philosophy after his ordination to the priesthood. His bishop, recognizing his unusual talent, sent him to the Jagellonian University in Cracow, where he studied modern and contemporary philosophy more deeply than any other modern pope. He was especially fascinated by the personalist philosophy of the German Catholic thinker Max Scheler (1874–1928), who, in important ways, strongly influenced the young Karol Wojtyla's understanding of the human person, as Wojtyla himself attests. Even as Auxiliary Bishop of Cracow, and later as Archbishop of Cracow, he wrote and published one philosophical study after another on the human person and on the moral life. He wrote a major treatise on personalist philosophy called *The Acting Person*. He held the chair in ethics at the Catholic University in Lublin up until the time of

his election as pope. In his years as Bishop of Cracow he found time to offer various courses in ethics
and personalist philosophy in Lublin. He was, then,
the pope to write the encyclical *Fides et Ratio*. And
he is *the* pope to teach us about all that philosophy
can give us Christians for the understanding of the
human person.

Notice that Pope John Paul II teaches us by his
example as well as by what he writes. His work in
philosophy is not like a hobby, something he has pur-
sued next to his work as pastor. As we have seen,
it enters everywhere into his teaching as pope. He
would not be the pope he is but for his deep forma-
tion in philosophy. His way of articulating the truth
about the human person and of giving prophetic
witness to the dignity of the person is profoundly
formed by his philosophy of the person. He gives an
example to the whole Church by the way in which
he brings together faith and philosophical reason in
himself.

Some of you may be eager to read about Pope
John Paul's personalist philosophy but may be un-
clear as to just what philosophy is. It is a sign of the
eclipse of philosophy in our time that many intel-
ligent people no longer know what it is. I won't

try right now to give you an abstract definition of philosophy, but rather will offer what is called an ostensive definition. That is, in the subsequent chapters I'll raise questions of personalist philosophy and discuss them philosophically with you. From these discussions you will gather what philosophy is and will then understand why it has always had a special place in the life of the Church.

Others of you may feel intimidated at the thought of studying philosophy. You may have the idea that philosophy is very difficult to understand and can be studied by only a few highly trained specialists. And it's true that some of Pope John Paul's writings are not easy to read and understand. But basic ideas of philosophy can be stated simply; philosophy can be brought into the marketplace as old Socrates did. The basic ideas of John Paul's personalism are meant for a broad audience.

Chapter Two

WORTHY OF RESPECT: THE PERSONALIST NORM

Back when he was still Archbishop of Cracow, Pope John Paul II once wrote to his friend, the great theologian Henri de Lubac: "I devote my very rare free moments to a work that is close to my heart and is devoted to the metaphysical sense and mystery of the person. The evil of our times consists in the first place in a kind of degradation, indeed in a pulverization, of the fundamental uniqueness of each human person."

Here is the center of gravity of Pope John Paul II's mind and of his thought: the mystery of each human person. How shall we enter into his philosophical reflection on persons? Let's look into his moral philosophy, and in particular that part of it where he formulates the first principle of morality.

The personalist norm

Moral philosophers have always sought out the most basic principles of the moral life. They have come up with principles such as "care for your soul," "provide for your full flourishing and well-being," "live according to nature," "give to everyone what is due to him," "fulfill the commands of God," "do unto others as you would have them do unto you." But only in the last few centuries have moral philosophers expressed the first principles in distinctly personalist terms. The German philosopher Immanuel Kant (1724–1804) led the way when he formulated the first principle of morality: "Persons should always be treated as their own ends and should never be merely used as an instrumental means." This principle installs respect for persons at the center of the moral life, and it sees all using of persons as its principal violation.

Pope John Paul II is profoundly indebted to this new personalism in ethics. In his first book, *Love and*

Responsibility, he writes: "This personalist norm, in its negative aspect, states that the person is the kind of good which does not admit of use and cannot be treated as an object of use and as the means to an end." Then he goes beyond Kant and adds: "In its positive form the personalist norm says that the person is a good toward which the only proper and adequate attitude is love."

This personalist norm provides us with a most helpful entry into the pope's thought; once we get acquainted with the norm, we are naturally led to ask what exactly it means to say that each person is "his own end," and what it means to "use" others.

Pope John Paul II answers by teaching that each person possesses himself or belongs to himself. Persons are not just there, like rocks or plants; they are handed over to themselves, they are their own. As a result, they can make different things of themselves, they can accept or reject themselves. Above all, they can determine themselves in freedom, indeed, in a certain sense, they can create themselves. If you try to use a person as a mere instrument, then you deprive that person of the space he needs for the uniquely personal work of self-creation. If we are really going to respect persons, then we must step back from them, take our heavy hands off them, and let them be, that is, live as self-determining beings. In respecting them like this and in abstaining from all using, we treat persons as their own end.

Here we have the reason why it is wrong to own another human being as property, as is attempted in the institution of slavery. As a person the other belongs to himself and so cannot belong to someone else as property. Trying to own the other violates the other precisely as a self-possessing person.

Objection to the idea that persons belong to themselves

Religiously committed people are likely to balk at the idea that we belong to ourselves. They may say that we do not belong to ourselves but to God, and that we are not our own end but that God is our end, and that there is no indignity in being used as an instrument in God's hands ("Lord, make me an instrument of your peace"). In other words, they may find something downright impious about the central intuition of Pope John Paul II's personalism! Let us ask what God thinks about our existing as our own ends, for He surely has the last word on what is impious and what is not. Pope John Paul II interprets the mind of God for us like this:

> Nobody can use a person as a means toward an end, no human being, nor yet God the Creator. On the part of God, indeed, it is totally out of the question, since, by giving man an intelligent and free nature, He has thereby ordained that each man alone will decide for himself the ends of his activity, and not be a blind tool of someone else's ends. Therefore, if God intends to direct man toward certain goals, He allows him, to begin with, to know those goals, so that he may make them his own and strive toward them independently.

He says "strive toward them independently" because once we understand the goals that God proposes to us, we can will these all on our own. He doesn't have to trick us or coerce us into moving toward those goals, as if we were mere instruments for His purposes. He deals with us as persons by enabling us to want them for ourselves just as much as He wants them for us. He treats us as partners in His work rather than as instruments for achieving it.

Human persons, then, commit no impiety by respecting each other as beings who belong to themselves and exist as their own ends, for God shows us just this respect. Indeed, Pope John Paul II says in another place that we share in God's vision of us human beings when we respect each other as ends and abstain from all using of each other.

We belong to God, not as the plants and animals belong to Him, but as human persons, who in some sense also belong to ourselves. We persons are able consciously and freely to enact our belonging to God by handing ourselves over to Him, and in this way we come to belong to God far more perfectly than any sub-personal creature; but we achieve this more perfect belonging precisely on the basis of our belonging ourselves. As for the religious talk of gladly being an instrument in the hands of God, Pope John Paul II suggests that we should interpret this as the unconditional readiness to serve God, but he reminds us that such unconditional service must be offered in a manner appropriate to our being persons, which means that our service must not include the readiness to "be a blind tool of someone else's ends." God is the very last one who would ask for such a violation of the personhood that He Himself created.

The idea that God knows better than anyone else that we are our own ends and are never rightly used as mere means, was expressed at Vatican II. In the Pastoral Constitution on the Church in the Modern World (*Gaudium et Spes*), which Archbishop Karol Wojtyla had a large hand in drafting, we find this sentence, which Pope John Paul II cannot quote often enough: Although man is "the only creature on earth that God has wanted for its own sake," it is nevertheless true that man "can fully discover his true self only in a sincere giving of himself." I will return in this book to the second part of this sentence; for now I want to focus on the personalist affirmation that man is "the only creature on earth that God has wanted for its own sake." God does not will the plants and animals for their own sakes; He rather wills them for the sake of human persons (which does not mean, however, that plants and animals are mere instrumental means for us). But human persons He wills for no one else's sake: He wills them for their own sake, which means that they must exist as their own ends.

Living the personalist norm in our lives

One might object that it is impossible to live by the personalist norm. One might say that whenever an employer hires an employee for a job, he is using the employee as a means for getting the job done, but what reasonable person would say that you violate personal dignity by the very act of hiring someone to do a job? In other words, there must be something wrong with the personalist norm, since it seems to condemn as immoral the most normal economic relations.

To this Pope John Paul II responds that the relation between employer and employee is indeed fraught with the danger that the employee will be treated only as a means, and that when this happens the relation is indeed morally out of order. But he goes on to say that the relation need not be one of mere using. The employer can abstain from all coercion and intimidation in hiring people, he can abstain from deceptively enticing people to take a job, he can take account not only of "the bottom line" but of the good of the employees, he can even invite them to share somehow in the responsibility for the enterprise. In these and in other ways the employer—

employee relation can be "personalized," so that the employee is acknowledged as person even in the midst of this economic relation.

Pope John Paul II brings the personalist norm into every area of human life, and so it is not surprising that he has brought it into his rich teaching on man and woman. We will see later how fruitfully John Paul uses it to rethink the issues of sexual morality. He shows how the sexual behaviors traditionally regarded as wrong are wrong because persons get used in a degrading way. He shows that the requirements of chastity are nothing other than the requirements of the personalist norm as applied to man–woman relations. In this personalist way he achieves, as we shall see, a particularly convincing and winning affirmation of Christian sexual morality.

Chapter Three

THE INTERIORITY OF HUMAN PERSONS

St. Augustine is famous for warning us not to lose ourselves in the world outside and for admonishing us to turn within, to enter into the "inner man." He explores the interiority of man like no one before him did. Now Pope John Paul II is likewise fascinated with the interiority of persons. He announces one of the great themes of his personalist philosophy when he writes: "We can say that the person as a subject is distinguished from even the most advanced animals by a specific inner self, an inner life, characteristic only of persons. It is impossible to speak of the inner life of animals." As we study the interiority of persons in this chapter, we will go more deeply into the aspect of personhood that we studied in the last chapter, namely, each person as his or her own end.

Looking from within

Let us consider the way in which we know the world around us—plants, rocks, clouds, stars, houses, animals, and other human beings. We know them all as objects of our experience, that is, as standing in front of us, as outside of us. But we know ourselves in a fundamentally different way; we do not just stand in front of ourselves, looking at ourselves from the outside. Rather, we first experience ourselves in the more intimate way of being present to ourselves, that is, we first experience ourselves not from without but from within, not as object but as subject, not as something presented to us but as a subject that is present to itself. Now this self-presence is the interiority of a human person.

A rock has an inner side, which is revealed when the rock is split, but this inner side has nothing to do with interiority. For the only way the inside of the rock can be experienced is as the object of someone's experience, it does not experience itself from within itself. The inside of the rock is as external as the outer surface of it; the rock is incapable of that dimension of being that we call interiority.

This interior self-presence, in which each person dwells with himself, is easy to overlook. When we think about something, give attention to it, or talk about it, we put it in front of ourselves, and so it is natural to think that this is the way we experience even ourselves. Of course, we can make an object of ourselves, as when we tell someone about our feelings, but our primary experience of ourselves is not from without as object but from within as subject, and so this self-experience is in a way hidden from our view.

Now Pope John Paul II teaches that we must take account of our interiority if we are to do justice to ourselves as persons. He says that for too long philosophy tried to understand man apart from interiority. Even the great Aristotle (385–322 B.C.) looked at man mainly from the outside, examining man in the same way he examined plants and animals. He used the same categories for explaining man and the other beings in nature, categories such as substance or matter/form. His cosmological approach to man, as Pope John Paul II calls it, still allowed him to see that man ranks higher than plants and animals, but he was not able to do full justice to man as person. Only the exploration of interiority that begins with St. Augustine discloses the mystery of each human being as person.

An example

Here is a striking example that we can gather from the writings of Pope John Paul II. If we look at the sexual union of man and woman from the outside, that is, from a cosmological perspective, we notice primarily the procreative power of it. As a result, we are struck by the similarity between the sexual union among human beings and the sexual union among those sub-human animals that reproduce by means of the coupling of male and female. One sees why Pope John Paul II says that the cosmological perspective tends to "reduce man to the world," that is, to stress the continuity of human and non-human beings.

Let us now bring in the factor of interiority. Let us ask how man and woman experience their marital intimacy from within, as only they can experience it. The answer: They experience something that has no counterpart among the animals and is entirely distinct from the procreative potential of their union; they *experience themselves making a gift of themselves to each other in their spousal intimacy.* This self-donation marks a radical difference between human and sub-human animal sexuality; it underlies the discontinuity rather than the continuity between them. For self-donation is not apparent to one looking in on man and woman from the outside; only one who knows something of the interiority of man and woman can find this entirely new dimension of sexual union. We could say that spousal self-donation is cosmologically invisible; only those who dwell in the world of interiority can find it.

Here is the point that Pope John Paul II wants to make as a philosopher: We get a more personalist understanding of the sexual union of man and woman by looking into their interiority and bringing to light their will to self-donation. In giving myself to another I not only participate in a cycle of nature that resembles other animals, but I also perform an eminently personal act. If we remain content with the cosmological perspective, seeing nothing more in sexual union than its procreative potential, then our understanding of it is incomplete.

Of course, Pope John Paul II does not propose that the personalist perspective should replace the cosmological perspective. Man is not exclusively a being of interiority. We will study later the rich philosophy of personal embodiment in Pope John Paul II. The cosmological perspective retains for him its own truth; the task is to keep it from being our only perspective and to enrich it with the experience of interiority.

We find another striking instance of Pope John Paul II's interest in personal interiority in his profound commentary on the passage in Genesis 1 that deals with the creation of man and woman. He remarks that there are in fact two accounts of the creation of man and woman in Genesis 1 and that one of them is more "subjective" than the other. He means that one of them stresses the self-experience of Adam and Eve—the *solitude* of Adam before the creation of Eve, the *shame* of Adam and Eve after their fall—more than the other. In other words, one stresses the interiority of Adam and Eve more than the other does. He focuses most of his commentary on the more subjective or interior passage because it lends more support to his personalist interpretation of man and woman.

Subjectivity vs. subjectivism

One might be perplexed at Pope John Paul II using "subjective" in a positive sense. We are used to
the term "subjective" being used as a term of rebuke
and "objective" being used approvingly. But among
many philosophers "subjective" and "subjectivity"
take on a very positive sense when they are used to
express interiority. When Pope John Paul II speaks
with enthusiasm about the subjectivity of persons, as
he often does, he is not making any concessions to
"subjectivism," which is the destructive philosophy
that reduces reality to my feeling and experiencing
of it. Pope John Paul II does not mean that a person
is nothing more than his self-experience, only that
self-experience reveals like nothing else the mystery
of each human being as person.

We are now in a position to see that there is
something distinctly modern about the thought of
Pope John Paul II. It is often said that modern philosophy begins with the new interest in personal
subjectivity that emerges in the seventeenth century.
Pope John Paul II is a full participant in this "turn to
the subject" and is in fact indebted to it. Even though
he completely rejects subjectivism, he does not let
the fear of subjectivism prevent him from turning

his attention to the subjectivity, or interiority, of human beings, so as to understand better what it means to say that they are persons.

Here we have an explanation of Pope John Paul II's interest in that movement of thought known as phenomenology. As a student of philosophy, he immersed himself in the German phenomenologist Max Scheler, whose work, as he tells us, deeply formed his mind in certain ways. While it is not easy to explain phenomenology in a few words, we can say this much: The phenomenologist practices in a disciplined way an unconditional respect for all that is revealed in experience; he therefore takes very seriously the experience of subjectivity, or interiority.

Let us conclude by referring to the passage in Vatican II's *Gaudium et Spes* where mention is made of personal interiority: "Man is not deceived when he regards himself as superior to bodily things and as more than just a speck of nature or a nameless unit in the city of man. For *by his interiority* he rises above the whole universe of mere objects" (no. 14).

The is just what John Paul II has tried to elaborate in his personalist philosophy: The dignity of man as person, whereby he surpasses everything in the cosmos, is disclosed to us in the mystery of each person's interiority.

Chapter Four

PERSONS ARE UNREPEATABLE

A person is always more than a mere instance of a type

We know how dangerous it is to think of human beings in terms of general types or patterns. We think of someone as a typical Serb, a typical woman, a typical adolescent. If we think that this is all there is to them, that there is nothing else of significance about them besides being a typical this or that, then we lose sight of them as persons. We have only to consider the point of view of people who are viewed through the lens of general types and patterns; they feel ignored as persons. Just when I think someone is taking a personal interest in me, I painfully realize that the interest is based only on my being a typical something or other. This means that the one taking the interest in me would take the same interest in any other equally typical man or woman, and so his interest is not really in me as a person. In other words, I am replaceable in his eyes by any other equally good instance of the type that interests him. This is why I feel offended: I know that as a person I am in fact more than just a replaceable instance of a type.

There are, of course, beings that really are nothing more than replaceable instances of a type. Take, for example, the thousands of copies of a book. Each is only an instance of the book. If you lose the copy that you just bought, you can completely recover your loss by getting another copy; you will find everything in the second copy that you had looked for in the first. Any one copy completely replaces any other copy of a given issue.

With persons it is just the opposite: No person is replaceable by any other, because no person exists in the first place as a mere instance or specimen of a type or pattern. This amazing irreplaceability, or unrepeatability, lies at the heart of what it is to be a person. This truth receives particular attention in the personalism of Pope John Paul II. It is closely connected with the interiority of persons and also with each person being his or her own end, aspects of personhood discussed in previous chapters. Pope John Paul II writes:

> We speak of individual animals, looking upon them simply as single specimens of a particular animal species. And this definition suffices. But it is not enough to define a man as an individual of the species Homo sapiens. And why not? Because each human being is more than just an instance of the human kind; we do not know a human being as person if we know him only in terms of that which is common to all human beings.

The Holy Father continues:

> The term "person" has been coined to signify that a man cannot be wholly contained within the concept "individual member of the species," but that there is something more to him, a particular richness and perfection in the manner of his being which can only be brought out by the use of the word "person."

This "something more" is what makes each person unrepeatably himself or herself.

Unrepeatability and immortality

Let us bring in here the great philosophical question of whether an individual human being in any sense lives on after death. Now if each of us were just a specimen of the human kind, if this were the whole truth about each, then there would be no point in any individual human being living on without end; an unending succession of different human individuals would provide all the continuity of existence that could be desired. If we want roses, for example, to continue in existence, it is quite enough to have an unending succession of roses; there is no need that this or that individual rose should never die. It is only because human beings have a different relation to their species than roses have to theirs, only because each human being is more than an instance of the human kind, more than a mere specimen of any particular type or quality, but rather a person, unrepeatably himself or herself, that each individual human being ought to exist forever. If a person were to go out of existence altogether then something would be lost to the world that could never be recovered in any subsequent person. Humanity would suffer an irretrievable loss. This loss is averted not by there being an unending succession of human beings, but only by the continued existence of each individual human person.

The ineffability of each person

Here is a good way of recognizing this mysterious unrepeatability of each human person. The more you come to know and love some person, the less you find yourself able to express what it is that you know and love. You find something in the other that is unutterable, ineffable, unspeakable. You can describe well enough the various qualities of the other, the types and kinds that he falls under, but there is something else, something deeper in the other that escapes your expressive and descriptive powers. You see and experience this "something else" as you come to know and love the other as person, but you cannot render it in clear concepts, and you just stammer when you try. What you are encountering is precisely the other as unrepeatable person. The problem is that our language is suited to expressing only properties that are common to many; it fails us when we try to give expression to that which is unrepeatably some person's own.

A famous French writer once said: "If I am entreated to say why I loved him, I feel that this cannot be expressed except by answering, 'Because it was he, because it was I.'" This is, of course, not much of an answer to the question why I love someone, but it's all we can say when we reach beyond the genus and species of the other, beyond all the qualities he has, beyond all the stereotypes that he fits, all the kinds that he belongs to, all the classes that he can be gathered into, and reach for the unrepeatable person that he is.

Here we have the reason for the awe that Pope John Paul II feels before each human person, and for the way he stresses *each human person, none excluded*, when he speaks of personal dignity. It all comes from his strong sense of the unrepeatability of each person. As everyone knows, Pope John Paul II has a particular concern for those who suffer, for the helpless, for the unborn. Whereas the world sees little in these people, since it is looking for outstanding instances of human qualities, Pope John Paul II bends down with the mind of Christ to each of them, acknowledging the unrepeatable person in each of them.

Connections with the previous chapters

Let us glance back at the second chapter, where we explained why each person is his or her own end and is never rightly used as a mere instrumental means. This is obviously closely akin to being unrepeatable. It makes little difference whether you violate persons by using them in a purely instrumental way, or by treating them as replaceable specimens. Sometimes these two ways of violating persons seem to coincide. For example, suppose an employer meets with someone applying for a job; if he sees the applicant only in terms of the job description, that is, only as a good or bad specimen of the job description, if he acknowledges nothing more in the applicant, then he is at one and the same time treating the applicant as replaceable and using the applicant as a mere means for the functioning of his enterprise. He is failing to treat the applicant both as one who is his own end and as one who is an unrepeatable person. For these are simply two aspects of what it is to be a person.

We can also cast a glance back at the interiority of persons. Recall how we distinguished between looking at someone from the outside and looking at someone from the inside. Well, as long as we look from the outside, talking about him in the third person, seeing him as an object, we tend to see him in terms of qualities that he has in common with many others. But as soon as we change perspectives and realize that this person has his own hopes and fears and sufferings, as soon as we practice a certain empathy toward him, entering into his interiority and understanding him when he says "I," then we see him as unrepeatable person. If the employer interviewing the applicant will only take a little interest in how the applicant experiences the world, a little interest in what makes him anxious and what makes him happy, he will begin to see the candidate as person. By being sensitive to the applicant's interiority, the employer begins to encounter him as unrepeatable person, and he prevents the interview from being depersonalizing for the applicant.

Of course, Pope John Paul II has no intention of belittling our common human nature. Through our common nature we exist in a profound solidarity with one another. As Christians we believe that human nature is the channel through which the redemptive work of Christ is communicated to us. Christ restored human nature in Himself, and we can be restored for the very reason that we share human nature with Him. Pope John Paul II affirms all of this in its place, but he also affirms that it is just as fundamental to Christian belief to say that persons are never mere instances or specimens of this common nature, for each person exists before God as if the only one.

Chapter Five

FREEDOM

Any philosopher who takes man seriously as person is sure to affirm the freedom of persons. There are, of course, no lack of philosophers who deny freedom—they are called "determinists"—but none of them ever makes a point of saying that human beings are persons. Personhood and freedom are inseparable. In his personalism Pope John Paul II has much to say about freedom, just as we would expect.

Acting through oneself

The first affirmation of Pope John Paul II on freedom is made in the form of a contrast. He contrasts individuals *being acted upon* by some cause, with individuals *acting through themselves*. When he explains being acted upon, he usually says that it is a matter of passively undergoing that which happens in a human being, or that which happens to a human being. For example, if I catch some infectious disease, I undergo the disease as it runs its course. It befalls me, and I am passive in relation to it. Suffering from the disease is not a matter of acting through myself, but of enduring something that happens in me. And a disease is only one example; there are obviously in me all kinds of impulses and appetites that, in their first stirring, happen only in me. Now Pope John Paul II wants to say that I do not really live as person when I endure that which happens in me; I am not revealed as the person I am by that which I passively undergo. Rather, it is only by acting through myself (perhaps in response to what I passively undergo) that I really live and thrive as person. This important truth is compactly expressed in the title of Pope John Paul II's major philosophical work, *The Acting Person*.

Here then is Pope John Paul II's first and most basic formula for the freedom of persons: acting through oneself. As for a striking example of such freedom, let us turn to a memorable passage in Robert Bolt's play about the life and death of St. Thomas

More, *A Man for All Seasons*. St. Thomas More says to Norfolk: "I will not give in because I oppose it—I do—not my pride, not my spleen, nor any other of my appetites but I do—I!" St. Thomas More is simply saying in the strongest possible terms that his refusal to give in to the king is not some instinctive reaction that only happens in him; his refusal is rather a matter of his acting through himself. He says "I" so emphatically just to express his acting through himself or, in other words, his "owning" his act of refusing the king. The passage continues with St. Thomas More going up to Norfolk and feeling him up and down and then saying: "Is there no single sinew in the midst of this that serves no appetite of Norfolk's but is just Norfolk? There is! Give that some exercise, my lord!" In other words, St. Thomas More challenges Norfolk not to be someone who is just acted upon and who just endures all the fears that befall him, but to be someone who acts through himself—someone who can say "I" and be called by his most personal name.

Once he has established this principle of his personalism, Pope John Paul II has parted ways once and for all from all forms of determinism. According to this philosophy, when I act it is not really I who act, but something else that acts through me, such as my genes or the neurons firing in my brain or other persons whom I have internalized; I am acted on by these forces in such a way as to be put out of commission as a person acting through himself. John Paul teaches that though I am subject to many such forces acting on me, I am also handed over to myself in such a way as to be able to determine myself in relation to these forces, and thus to assert my freedom in the face of them.

Freedom and the other aspects of the person

It is not difficult to see that this idea of persons acting through themselves fits perfectly with the aspects of persons discussed in the earlier chapters. Take interiority. A person shows his interiority most of all when he acts through himself. As long as he is dominated by what happens to him, he does not seem to live out of an inner center; he does not seem to be a subject but an object. But when someone says "I" in the vigorous tone of voice with which St. Thomas More says it, then he expresses his interiority.

Or, go back all the way to the second chapter, where we explained the idea of persons being their own ends and never existing as mere instruments. What does it mean to be one's own end? We can now add to what was said then: It means being the kind of being that can act through itself, determining itself in freedom. Why does it violate persons so seriously to use them as an instrumental means? Because in serving as a mere means, they are forced to become like an extension of the user and are thus deprived of the space they need for acting through themselves. If persons were incapable of acting through themselves, they would not exist as their own ends, and then they would not even be the kind of being that can be violated by being used.

Or what about the last chapter with its discussion of the unrepeatability of persons? Does a person not reveal the unrepeatable self that he is by the free choices he makes? If a person is always dominated by what happens in him and never succeeds in acting through himself, then his status as unrepeatable person remains hidden. He will even feel a painful anonymity in himself, as if he were only a specimen or instance of the forces surging through him. He can learn to say "I" in a way that expresses his unrepeatable self only by recovering his power of self-determination.

The truth about good

One of the great themes in the teaching of Pope John Paul II is what he calls the dependency of freedom on truth. He means that freedom has its own law or higher norm, which he calls "the truth about good." We cannot really act through ourselves if our acting is not based on respect for this truth about good.

Everyone knows from experience what happens to our freedom when we live "lawlessly," paying no heed to the truth about good and instead just grasping for what we want. There is a priceless sentence in Oscar Wilde's memoir of his earlier days of debauched living. He says: "I ceased to be captain of my soul." He means that he was unable to act through himself because he refused to live by the truth about good. In other words, he lived in a most servile condition because he lived abandoned to his cravings and wants. All kinds of addictive patterns, inner demons, and contradictory motives take over in the soul of the person who scorns the truth about good. As a result, such a person is crippled in his ability to act through himself. On the other hand, the person who lives by the truth about good never complains about being disabled as a person, about being deprived of the captaincy of his soul, and, in fact, he experiences himself as empowered by the truth about good really to act through himself. St. Thomas More can say "I" so emphatically only because he acknowledges in all of his action the requirements of good and right. He is as free as he is, eminently the captain of his soul, only because he is unconditionally ready to fulfill these requirements, whatever they demand of him.

And yet, many contemporary men and women are afraid of the truth about good. They want freedom on their own terms. They see in the truth about good, which is the law for their freedom, a threat to their freedom. They fear that a higher law not of their own making can only interfere with their acting through themselves and hence interfere with them as persons. They claim that they would lose their individuality if they were to submit to a law that is the same for all persons. And so they think that to save themselves as persons they have to become subjectivists about good, that is, people who think that each person creates his or her own conception of good and of the moral life.

Pope John Paul II is sensitive to this fear that so many feel in the face of the objective truth about good. He understands it, and he goes to great trouble to respond to it. In our next chapter, we will see how Pope John Paul II defends the law of our freedom and shows that we can be fully free in no other way than in living by this law.

Chapter Six

FREEDOM AND TRUTH

We live as persons by acting through ourselves in freedom: This is the aspect of Pope John Paul II's personalism that we examined in the last chapter. John Paul also teaches that there is a law of freedom, which he calls the "truth about good." Though people are afraid that this law will interfere with their freedom, it is in fact the basis for living in freedom, as we shall try to show in the present chapter.

Coercion vs. persuasion

Let us suppose that some zealous Christians come into an area where the native people have never heard of Christianity, and that they proceed to force these people to profess the Christian faith and to live the Christian life. The coerced converts would be living in accordance with the objective truth all right, but they would not be liberated by the truth. They would feel oppressed by Christianity, even though it is the very truth of God. The problem, of course, is that their own judgment has been by-passed; they have not been given a chance to see the truth of Christianity for themselves. So this is the first thing to understand about John Paul's "truth about good": It empowers us to act freely only if we understand it and choose it on the basis of under-standing it; if it is imposed on us, then it interferes with our freedom. It is, then, the "understood truth about good" that is the correctly expressed law of our freedom.

One sees why John Paul in his encyclical on the missionary activity of the Church says that the Church does not go out to the nations to *impose* re-vealed truth on them, but to *propose* it to them. Only in this way does the truth about good become the friend of the freedom of persons. In general John Paul distinguishes in his personalism between coer-cion and persuasion. Though coercion is sometimes unavoidable in human affairs, John Paul nevertheless wants coercion to be replaced by persuasion as far as possible. He often reflects on the particular respect shown to persons when we make a point of influencing them by means of persuasion. For if we give them a good reason for acting in a certain way, a reason that they can understand, then they now have as much a motive for acting in that way as we ourselves do. Their acting in that way is not an extension of our acting, as it is when we coerce them, but is truly their own act. If there were no such thing as the truth about good, there would be no such thing as persuasion; we could influence each other only by way of coercion.

Let us see how John Paul practices what he preaches. We all know how deeply committed he is to the teaching of the Church on the objective evil of contraception, as set forth in the encyclical *Humanae Vitae*. But he has not tried to uphold this teaching simply by "laying down the law," by threatening punishments, and the like. He thinks that that is just the approach that makes the moral law seem to people to cramp their freedom. He takes a different approach. On one occasion he said: "It is not enough that this encyclical be faithfully and fully proposed, *but it also is necessary to devote oneself to demonstrating its deepest reasons*." He knows that the teaching of the encyclical is rooted in the truth about man and woman, and he wants nothing more than to make this truth understandable to the people of our time.

If we do not succeed in understanding this truth, then the Church's prohibition of contraception will seem to us to be outside of us and will be experienced as an imposition. But if we understand how this teaching grows out of the truth about man and woman, and how we *live in the truth of our own being* by living in accordance with the teaching, then we internalize it, that is, we make it our own. As a result, we are fully free in living it, even when it requires considerable sacrifice from us. In his major philosophical treatise, John Paul reflects on this process of making the truth our own, and says: "The tension arising between the objective order of norms and the inner freedom of the person is relieved by truth, by the conviction of the truthfulness of good. But this tension is, on the contrary, intensified and not relieved, by external pressures, by the power of injunction and compulsion."

Hence the supreme pastoral importance of showing forth in a convincing way the truthfulness of the moral norms taught by the Church. John Paul takes the faithful seriously as persons by leading them beyond blind obedience and educating them to the rational obedience that makes them free.

This of course does not mean that a Catholic is excused from a moral teaching of the Church that he does not yet fully understand. It just means that the faithful, if they want to live in freedom, should do everything they can to develop their understanding of the moral norms taught by the Church, and that the Church for her part should do all that she can to support this development of understanding.

The divine pedagogy

John Paul often dwells on the fact that God Himself wants human persons to understand the truth they live by. He does not make them blind instruments of His plans, but reveals to them something of His counsels so as to make them His collaborators. Here is a striking example of the personalist pedagogy that John Paul detects in God. In his book *Crossing the Threshold of Hope* he asks in one chapter, "Why is there so much evil in the world?" He begins his answer saying: "One response could be that God does not need to justify Himself to man. It is enough that He is omnipotent. From this perspective everything

He does or allows must be accepted. This is the position of the biblical Job."

But John Paul is not satisfied with this response, and so he proceeds to suggest a very different one: "But God, who besides being Omnipotence is Wisdom and Love, desires to justify Himself to mankind." That is an absolutely extraordinary statement, the likes of which I have never seen in a Catholic writer: "God desires to justify Himself to mankind"! That is, God wants man to cry out, "Why, O God, why?" when man suffers; He wants man to understand something of the divine meaning of the suffering that afflicts him, and to live in the freedom that comes from this understanding.

John Paul is bound to think of John 15:15 when he presents this part of his personalist philosophy: "No longer do I call you servants, for the servant does not know what his master is doing; but I have called you friends, for all that I have heard from my Father I have made known to you." In taking us as friends and not servants, Christ also takes us as persons, making us free in the truth that He reveals to us.

Non-violence

We said that people are afraid of the truth about good because they think it will cramp their freedom. They are also afraid of it because they think that those who have strong convictions concerning the truth about good are sure to resort to coercion against those who disagree with them about this truth. The fear is that if you think you know something about the truth about good, you are bound to be intolerant of all those who deny the truth that you affirm. You can be tolerant toward your neighbors only if you doubt that there is any such thing as truth about good.

We have already given one response to this objection: If we really believe in the truth that we profess, and really believe that it is knowable to all people of good will, then we are in a position to propose that truth gently and to abstain from all coercion. Here is another response based not on theory but on history. John Paul sees great significance in the fact that the Communist establishment in Poland was brought down not by the force of arms, nor by any kind of violence, but by the moral witness of the Polish workers to the truth. In a situation where many thought that nothing but force would avail, one was able to achieve a complete victory by appealing to the consciences of the adversaries. John Paul has written:

> The fall of this kind of bloc or empire was accomplished almost everywhere by means of peaceful protest, using only the weapons of truth and justice. While Marxism held that only by exacerbating social conflicts was it possible to resolve them through violent confrontation, the protests which led to the collapse of Marxism tenaciously insisted on trying every avenue of negotiation, dialogue, and witness to the truth, appealing to the conscience of the adversary and seeking to reawaken in him a sense of shared human dignity.

> The truth about good, far from necessarily leading to intolerant coercion, provides the only real alternative to all such coercion; it makes possible the act whereby one person appeals to the truth about good in dispute with another person, trying gently to persuade the other. This appeal can even be made to one's enemy, who can be challenged in his conscience and can be spiritually overcome by the force of the truth about good.

Chapter Seven

SELF-DONATION

Personalist philosophy can go astray in different ways; in the contemporary world it commonly goes astray by becoming too individualistic. This happens when I think of persons too much in terms of the rights with which each person is armed, and when I think of others mainly as potential intruders into my sphere of rights, so that I approach them with suspicion and mistrust. As an individualist of this kind, I think that people around me who suffer are none of my concern as long as I have not violated any of their rights. I acknowledge no responsibility for them as long as I have not assumed responsibility by entering into some kind of contract with them. This individualism is extremely widespread and affects all of us far more than we realize.

Now it may seem that we were lending support to this individualism in the earlier chapters. After all, we said that each person belongs to himself, is his own end, exists in some sense for his own sake, is unrepeatable, and acts as person by acting through himself. This may seem to be a philosophy that takes persons to be individuals in the individualistic sense. It may even seem that the individualistic isolation of persons from each other follows with a certain logic from all that was said in our first chapters about the "selfhood" of persons.

Mutual self-giving

The personalism of Pope John Paul II knows nothing of this individualism. He is in fact a sharp critic of it. In his personalism self-donation is as centrally important for persons as selfhood; solidarity with others is as centrally important as self-possession. He often reflects on the *polarity* of a person, that is, on the way in which a person is gathered into his own interiority and yet at the same time exists toward others, being called to share his being with them.

This polarity is admirably expressed in the Vatican II's Pastoral Constitution on the Church in the

Modern World (no. 24), which Pope John Paul II has quoted more times than anyone can count: Although man is "the only creature on earth that God has wanted for its own sake," it is nevertheless true that man "can fully discover his true self only in a sincere giving of himself." In our first chapters we explained selfhood, in virtue of which God wants man for his own sake; now we have to complete the image of the human person by examining "the sincere giving of himself" whereby a person "discovers himself."

Man and woman

Whenever Pope John Paul II discusses our vocation to self-donation, he inevitably brings up the division of human beings into man and woman. He thinks that by existing as man and woman, our vocation to self-donation is inscribed in our nature. He thinks that we are lifted out of our isolation and ordered to one another by existing as man and woman. Of course, it is not only by means of the gender difference that we are called to mutual self-giving; persons of the same gender can make a sincere gift of themselves in their relations with each other. But one of the primary ways in which we exist for each other is by existing as man and woman. It is also the way of existing for each other that particularly fascinates Pope John Paul II; the gender difference occupies a central place in his personalist philosophy.

If you take the difference between man and woman to be a merely biological difference, an arrangement of nature for the propagation of the human species, analogous to what nature does in the case of other animal species, then this difference loses its importance for personalist philosophy. For then human persons are genderless persons, gender making itself felt only at the lower, biological level. Pope John Paul II, by contrast, takes a radically personalist approach to man and woman; the gender difference is for him not only a biological but also a personal difference; it modifies human beings not only as animals but also and above all as persons. This is why the man–woman difference, and the way in which man and woman are turned to each other, is highly significant for Pope John Paul II's personalism; it reveals the vocation of human persons to self-donation.

The love between man and woman

We can see just how deep the gender difference is for Pope John Paul II if we consider how it underlies a unique kind of human love, the love between man and woman. In one very significant passage of his early work *Love and Responsibility*, Pope John Paul II asks what distinguishes this love from all other kinds of love, such as the love between siblings, or of children for their parents. He answers that it is a radical self-giving, which goes so far that one can speak of a self-surrender of the man and the woman to each other. They hand themselves over to each other in a manner that occurs in no other kind of human love; only in the love between man and woman do persons want to make themselves belong to each other. Not even the most self-sacrificing love of a mother for her child involves this gesture of self-surrender by the mother to the child. This is why a mother can love several children with full maternal love, but a man can love only one woman at a time, and a woman only one man at a time.

Of course, all love involves self-giving, or self-donation, but the love between man and woman involves it in an eminent way, so that this love is a particularly perfect kind of love—"the fullest, the most uncompromising form of love," Pope John Paul II says. This is why it is natural to study human love with constant reference to the particular form of love that is the love between man and woman.

A personalist objection

But a difficulty arises now in the minds of readers who remember all that was said about personal self-hood in the earlier chapters. We said that each person belongs to himself and has to be respected as his own end; how is it possible for such a being to give himself away to another and make himself belong to another? You do not have to be one of those extreme individualists mentioned above in order to wonder how a being that belongs to itself can make itself belong to another without abolishing itself as a being belonging to itself. This difficulty goes right to the heart of the issue that concerns us in this chapter: Is self-donation appropriate to persons? Do they flourish in living lives of self-donation, or do they destroy themselves as persons? Do they really have a vocation to self-donation?

Pope John Paul II's twofold response to this objection reveals the heart of his personalism. First, he says that man and woman can make a gift of themselves *for the very reason that they belong to themselves as persons.* An animal cannot practice any kind of self-giving *for the very reason that it does not belong to itself as person.* Since an animal is not gathered into itself with its own interiority, is not handed over to itself, it cannot "do" something with itself such as give itself in love. It acts and reacts, but does not hold itself in its hands so as to make a gift of itself. It follows, then, that belonging to another in love is not opposed to belonging to oneself as person; just the contrary, we are empowered by our belonging to ourselves to give ourselves to another in love (whether this be the love between man and woman or some other kind of love). Indeed, we understand what it means to belong to ourselves as persons only by also understanding the capacity for self-giving love that comes with belonging to ourselves.

Pope John Paul II gives a second response to the objection. He says that the world of persons is a world all its own, governed by laws unlike the laws governing the non-personal world. A non-personal being that imparts something of itself to another being is thereby diminished; a person who gives himself or herself in love thereby flourishes as person. By a great paradox of personhood, persons never belong so truly to themselves as when they give themselves away.

Here, then, is Pope John Paul II's response to the individualistic personalism mentioned at the outset. It wrongly thinks that persons can be their own ends, belonging to themselves as persons, only if they clutch at their being, jealously guarding it against the intrusions of others; but the personalism of Pope John Paul II thinks that persons can really live as their own ends only by giving and receiving themselves in love, whether they do this as man and woman or in some other way.

Chapter Eight

EMBODIMENT

I began my last chapter by saying that personalist philosophy can go astray in different ways, and I proceeded to show how in the contemporary world it commonly goes astray by becoming too individualistic. Now I want to begin the present chapter by mentioning a deviant form of personalism that will come as a surprise to most of my readers: Personalism also commonly goes astray by becoming too "spiritualistic." What could I possibly mean by this?

An overly spiritualistic personalism

Here is an example. A notorious "Catholic" feminist was recently calling into question all of the moral teachings of the Church in the area of sexuality, and she said, "God does not care what we do with each other's bodies; He only cares whether we treat each other as persons." In other words, men and women can do anything they like with each other's bodies—short of using coercion, of course—as long as they show respect for each other as persons. This in turn implies that there are no definite bodily ways of showing respect or disrespect for persons; showing respect to another is mainly an interior and disembodied act, since *any* use of another's body can in principle express respect. By detaching personal respect from its bodily expression, this feminist fails to understand how we exist as embodied persons. She thus provides a revealing example of what I call *spiritualism*. Since she lays great stress on showing respect for persons, her statement typifies spiritualistic personalism.

Now Pope John Paul II's personalism is very different: he takes very seriously the embodiment of human persons. He thinks that God cares very much what we do with each other's bodies. His personalism is not spiritualistic, it is incarnational.

The Holy Father's deepest thoughts on the embodiment of human persons are found in his discussion of man and woman, just as his deepest thoughts on the interpersonal vocation of human persons are found in his discussion of man and woman, as we saw in the last chapter.

According to the unisex view, the difference between man and woman is merely biological and not really personal. The main thing about man and woman is that they are both persons, their gender remaining outside of and below their personhood. They are genderless persons. Thus, from a personalist point of view, it does not much matter what a person's gender is; his or her capacity for interpersonal communion is unaffected by gender and other such bodily details. This unisex position tends to separate persons from their embodiment as man and woman.

You begin to get a sense for Pope John Paul II's incarnational personalism when you see how strongly he opposes the unisex position. He thinks that the personhood of a man is deeply formed by his being a man, no less than the personhood of a woman is deeply formed by her being a woman. In other words, human persons, being embodied, exist as masculine and feminine persons. Their embodiment as man and woman reaches into their personal existence, "ordaining" them to interpersonal communion.

Pope John Paul II even has a name for this capacity of the human body to serve love: He speaks of the "nuptial meaning" of the human body. He also speaks of a "sacramental" capacity the human body, which is capable of visibly expressing the invisible person, and of doing so in such a way as to invite persons to love each other. The point is that the pope takes our embodiment as man and woman far more seriously than does the unisex position, which is tainted by a spiritualistic personalism. A body endowed with a nuptial meaning and a sacramental power of rendering the invisible visible, is something far more and far richer than a merely biological body. It is a body endowed with rich personalist meaning, a body that mysteriously embodies the person.

Trinitarian perspective

In fact, Pope John Paul II here makes a bold theological point that strongly expresses his incarnational understanding of human persons. He says (and is the first pope to say) that the image of God can be detected in the man–woman difference. Since the Trinitarian God is a being of interpersonal communion, His creatures reflect Him in so far as they are beings of interpersonal communion; it follows that His human creatures reflect Him insofar as they exist as man and woman. Thus Pope John Paul II teaches that the image of God in human beings reaches into their bodily being. They do not reflect God just in being genderless spiritual persons, as the spiritualistic personalists think, but also in being embodied as man and woman.

How the nuptial meaning of the body gets obscured

Pope John Paul II also knows why the nuptial meaning of the human body is often ignored, so that the body is thought of in merely biological terms and the person is thought of in excessively spiritual terms.

First, the nuptial meaning of the body has been obscured by the fall, and as a result we often have great difficulty experiencing it. With extraordinary depth and originality, Pope John Paul II analyzes the way in which a man looks lustfully at the body of a woman. The body of the woman ceases to be expressive of her as person and to invite the man to spousal love. In this lustful looking, men see women, and in an analogous way women see men, as objects of consumption rather than as persons to be loved in a spousal way; their look violates the personhood of the other and ignores the fact that each person is "an enclosed garden," "a fountain sealed," expressions taken by Pope John Paul II from Song of Songs 4:12 and applied to men and women as persons.

It is on the basis of this analysis of concupiscence that Pope John Paul II made his famous statement back in 1980 that the "adultery in the heart" condemned by Jesus can be committed even by spouses within marriage. Though many were astonished by this claim, and others ridiculed it, it logically follows from his personalistic theology of the body. Depersonalizing lust may dominate the intimate relations of married spouses. When it does, they desire each other in such a way as to show disrespect for each other, and the fact that they are married does nothing to prevent such disrespect. Pope John Paul II teaches that marriage is not supposed to be a state of "legalized lust," but rather a state in which lust is overcome by love, and in which the selfish "sex appeal" of the body gives way to the deeper appeal of the nuptial meaning of the body.

There is something else that interferes with our experience of the body serving self-donation. Besides the selfish concupiscence of fallen men and women, there is also the modern passion to dominate the world and everything bodily by the means of technology. One looks upon the material world, and even one's own human body, as nothing but raw material for human making and manufacturing; everything in nature receives its meaning only from what man chooses to do with it. As a result, we become estranged from our body, looking at it as an object over against us. If we are hospitalized, we tend to become the object of medical treatment and cease to be the subject of our illness, as he puts it. We become unable to experience our bodies as sharing in our personal subjectivity, and we no longer recognize ourselves as embodied persons. We thus lose touch with the deep *personal* meanings—including the nuptial meaning—that are inscribed in our bodies.

The "redemption of the body," about which Pope John Paul II has much to say in his theology of the body, refers to the reintegration of bodily sexuality and personhood—the radical "personalization" of masculinity and femininity. The redemption of the body, though it will be consummated in eternity, begins already now in time. As this redemption is worked out, the body is drawn more and more into the lives of persons and made to serve more and more the love between persons.

Many people think that the Church holds in contempt the human body (especially its sexuality). But in fact, it is the non-Christian pagans who hold the body in contempt by taking the body as merely biological and by refusing to let it really embody persons. The spiritualistic feminist holds it in contempt when she says that God doesn't care what we do with each other's bodies. Pope John Paul II esteems the body far more than they do when he speaks of personalizing the body, of letting it reveal the person and serve as a sacrament of the person. You may be used to thinking that the problem with the secular world is that it makes too much of the body, but it is also true that it makes too little of the body. John Paul is *the* defender of the human body against its pagan detractors.

Chapter Nine

EMBODIMENT AND MORALITY

In the last chapter we got acquainted with John Paul's teaching on the embodiment of human persons. We saw how strongly he affirms the destiny of the human body to embody persons, to be personalized by them, that is, to be drawn up into the lives of persons. He does not speak of the body as something "merely biological," but speaks instead of its capacity to serve as a "sacrament" of the human person. As a result he appreciates the human body far more deeply than do those who only know how to use and manipulate it.

In the present chapter I propose to show how John Paul employs his personalist philosophy of embodiment to explain Christian morality. It is

not difficult to see that if you have a deficient understanding of embodiment you will not be able to
make sense of many norms and principles of morality. Recall the example given in the last chapter of a
dangerously disembodied understanding of persons:
"God doesn't care what we do with each other's
bodies, He only cares whether we treat each other
as persons." Little wonder that the feminist making
this statement was in the process of throwing out
almost all of the norms of Christian sexual morality.
On the other hand, John Paul, by doing justice to
the embodiment of persons, is able to throw fresh
new light on these norms, presenting them in a particularly convincing way.

In vitro fertilization

Let us consider the procedure in which sperm and
egg are extracted from the man and woman and
then brought together for fertilization in a laboratory dish, after which the fertilized egg is inserted into
the uterus of the woman, who hopefully becomes
pregnant. This sounds like the perfect medical procedure for infertile couples; and it seems to be not
an anti-life but a pro-life procedure, helping to bring

about conception where it would otherwise not oc-
cur. And yet John Paul rejected it in 1986 as morally
unacceptable. Why? Because he takes seriously the
embodiment of human persons.

In this procedure the bodies of the man and
woman are simply used as a source of biological
materials, which are assembled by a lab technician.
A new human person is in a way manufactured in
the laboratory. The nuptial meaning of the body is
bypassed. The man and woman do not enact their
love in and through their bodies; they simply present their bodies in the lab to have some gamete cells
extracted and then manipulated. The child does not
emerge from the enactment of their love, but is manufactured by a stranger. The child is made, not be-
gotten. The bodies of the parents, and of the child,
are too much the objects of manipulation; only people already deeply estranged from their bodies could
consider seriously such a procedure.

People who live their embodiment understand
that the one-flesh union of man and wife is simply
irreplaceable as the way of bringing a new human
person into being. They understand that the body of
a new person should not be assembled by a lab technician, who thereby comes to occupy a morally in-

tolerable position of superiority over the child. (He understandably feels that if he were entitled to make a person, he would also be entitled to "unmake" one, if, say, he has fertilized too many eggs.) Of course, it is not that these people idolize the "natural" way of achieving conception and have some irrational aversion to the artificiality of the in vitro method of achieving it, as if they were hankering after the simplicity of the pre-technological world. No, if the artificial method did not interfere with some great value of their embodiment, neither they nor John Paul would have any moral qualms about it.

Contraception

In the contraceptive mentality John Paul sees the same manipulative approach to the human body. Contracepting spouses think that they can sterilize the procreative potential of their marital intimacy while preserving the unitive power of it. They think they can take the mystery of marital intimacy apart, approaching it as a "cut and paste" operation on their computer, keeping what they want and excluding what they do not want. They are out of touch with their embodiment.

Those Catholic spouses who really live their embodiment understand that fertility is not an accident of marital intimacy; they experience in their bodies how the procreative meaning of their intimacy grows out of the unitive meaning of it. John Paul interprets for them the truth about their embodiment when he says that marital intimacy inevitably becomes poisoned with selfish using when its procreative potential is sterilized, and that the self-donation of the spouses is disrupted when they act to block the possibility of conception.

Sometimes people say the fertility of a man or woman is just a neutral biological fact, like the length of one's hair. Just as you are at liberty to cut your hair as short as you like it, you are at liberty to inhibit your fertility. The idea that it is wrong to manipulate your fertility seems to them as bizarre as the idea that it is unnatural to cut your hair. Sometimes people accuse John Paul of "physicalism," that is, of slavishly following natural physical tendencies instead of feeling at liberty to improve them for the good of persons.

Here is the response of John Paul. He agrees that there are plenty of neutral biological facts about the human body, and that we are indeed at liberty to change them. For instance, the fact that a cancer is naturally growing is no reason why we should not try to stop it. But he says that the very idea of considering the procreative power of human sexuality as just another biological fact shows that people are seriously estranged from their bodies. To do justice to fertility it is not enough to look at the body as an object; you have to live in your body with all its fertility and listen to what your body tells you about the intrinsic connection of spousal love and procreation. If only men and women could learn once again to dwell in their bodies and not always see their bodies as objects in a laboratory, they would readily understand what the Church teaches about the inseparability of the unitive and procreative meanings of the marital act.

"Fundamental option"

It is not only in particular moral issues like contraception that we can see people being estranged from their bodies; we can also see this estrangement in the way they think about the first principles of the moral life. John Paul gives us an example of this in his great encyclical on the moral life, *Veritatis Splendor* (1993), no. 65.

Many moral theologians separate the innermost moral freedom of persons from the concrete bodily actions that they perform. They say that we become morally good or bad according to the fundamental option that we make for or against God in the deepest depths of our freedom. The concrete actions that we perform do not make us good or bad; they are seen instead in terms of their impact on the world around us and not in terms of their impact on the moral character of the one who performs them. This means that you might, say, commit adultery without revoking your fundamental option for God and so without impairing the moral goodness of your character.

John Paul responds by acknowledging that there is indeed such a thing as a fundamental choice for or against God. But he insists that we human persons who exercise this choice are embodied persons, which means that we do not exercise it by withdrawing into a disembodied interiority; it is rather the case that we exercise it in and through our concrete bodily actions. Thus we unavoidably weaken or even revoke our decision for God by committing adultery or performing other seriously wrong actions. John Paul puts his finger on the deficient understanding of embodiment that he sees in these moral theologians: "To separate the fundamental option from concrete kinds of behavior means to contradict the substantial integrity or personal unity of the moral agent in his body and in his soul." And again: "It is in the unity of body and soul that the person is the subject of his own moral acts."

It was just one year after his election as pope that John Paul began his five-year cycle of addresses in which he presented to the Church his theology of the body. He seems to have sensed right from the beginning that the full truth about the embodiment of human persons would be of particular importance for his teaching as pope. He seems to have sensed, prophetically, that the moral confusion of our time derives in good part from the estrangement of persons from their bodies. He has been able to witness so powerfully to the truth about good and evil just because he began his ministry as pope by deeply re-thinking and reaffirming in his personalist way the embodiment of persons.

Chapter Ten

SOLIDARITY

"Solidarity" was not only the name of the famous Polish labor union that, inspired by the person and teaching of Pope John Paul II, precipitated the non-violent collapse of Communism in Poland and throughout Eastern Europe. Solidarity is also a term that expresses one of the great themes of Pope John Paul's Christian personalism.

Let us return to that extreme individualism discussed in a previous chapter. That is the view, you will recall, according to which persons are primarily possessors of rights, and *other* persons are primarily potential intruders into one's sphere of rights. The social ideal of this individualism is simply for persons to interact without anyone's rights getting violated. In that chapter we examined the personalist teaching that Pope John Paul opposes to this individualism, namely, his teaching on the self-donation of one person to another person, as of man and woman to each other.

But what about our life in economic society, or as members of our nation, or of the Church? Is there a place for self-donation not only in the I–Thou relation, but also in the we-relation of the larger communities to which we belong? Pope John Paul answers: The solidarity in which we stand in these communities invites us to new kinds of self-donation. Man as person is made for self-giving solidarity with others, and not for the social isolation that comes from the individualistic concern for one's rights.

Economic life

Pope John Paul has developed the social teaching of the Church in his three major social encyclicals. In them he repeatedly says that employers must not set up working conditions and hire workers exclusively with an eye to profit; they must also take account of their workers as human persons. He says that it is not enough to avoid violating the rights of workers; employers must also have some concern for the human wellbeing of their workers. In his philosophical language Pope John Paul puts it like this: There is an objective aspect of work (productivity) and a subjective aspect of work (the flourishing of the worker as human being), and managers should not be exclusively concerned with the former.

And why not? Because of the solidarity in which all human beings stand with each other. We are not ultimately strangers to each other, but exist as fellow human beings to each other. A manager who hires and fires only on the basis of profits and productivity is failing to live the truth about his solidarity with his workers. He thinks of himself as morally isolated from them, when in fact he has a certain co-responsibility for them.

And Pope John Paul adds this profound thought: The manager himself can thrive as person only if he lives his solidarity with his workers and accepts his co-responsibility for their well-being. He also says that it is not enough to exist *with* others; if you have really come into your own as person, you also have in some way to live *for* others. This holds for persons not only in their intimate relations with each other, but also in their socioeconomic relations.

Of course, Pope John Paul sees the danger of de-

personalized versions of social solidarity. Again and
again in the social encyclicals he denounces what he
calls "socialism," which sees "the individual person
simply as an element, a molecule within the social
organism, so that the good of the individual is completely subordinated to the functioning of the socioeconomic mechanism." A person can never exist as a
mere part in some whole, like a cell in an organism.
As we saw at the beginning, a person is his own end
and his own whole. So the solidarity in which we
stand with others must be understood as a way in
which we are bound together precisely *as persons.*

Ethnic hatred

It is not only economic injustice that moves the Holy
Father to remind men and women of the solidarity
in which we all exist; the terrible outbreaks of ethnic hatred that have occurred during his pontificate,
especially in Africa and the former Yugoslavia, have
also moved him in the same way.

In his important address to the United Nations
in 1995, he distinguishes between the universal and
the particular in the following way: Human nature is
universal, common to us all; it knits us together into

one human family. The ethnic and cultural identity of a people is something more particular, which is why there can be many different ethnic and cultural groups. The danger is that those in some particular group demonize those in some other group, forgetting the common humanity that unites them all. Pope John Paul said at the UN: "The fact of 'difference,' and the reality of 'the other' can sometimes be felt as a burden, or even as a threat. The fear of 'difference' can lead to a denial of the very humanity of the 'the other.'" And so the Holy Father has continually appealed to the consciences of warring peoples, reminding them of the human solidarity that remains intact in the midst of their ethnic differences.

The communion of sin

The Holy Father also explores solidarity in its deeper spiritual forms. In his 1984 apostolic exhortation, *Reconciliatio et Paenitentia,* he discusses "social sin," in the course of which he gives us this rich passage, worthy of close meditation:

> To speak of *social sin* means in the first place to recognize that, by virtue of human solidarity,

which is as mysterious and intangible as it is real
and concrete, each individual's sin in some way
affects others. This is the other aspect of that solidarity which on the religious level is developed
in the profound and magnificent mystery of the
communion of saints, thanks to which it has been
possible to say that "every soul that rises above
itself, raises up the world." To this *law of ascent*
there unfortunately corresponds the *law of de-
scent.* Consequently, one can speak of a *communion
of sin,* whereby a soul that lowers itself through
sin drags down with itself the Church and, in
some way, the whole world. In other words,
there is no sin; not even the most intimate and
secret one, the most strictly individual one, that
exclusively concerns the person committing it.
With greater or lesser violence, with greater or
lesser harm, every sin has repercussions on the
entire ecclesial body and the whole human family. (emphasis added)

It follows from this profound moral and spiritual
solidarity that we are all in some way co-responsible
for the evils around us. If only we were better, they
would be fewer. We should not condemn the evils

around us as if we had nothing to do with them, for then we would be yielding to the individualism mentioned above. Our solidarity with our fellow human beings is such that all the wrong that we do, and even if we do it in solitude, has a way of demoralizing all of them.

Solidarity in the Jubilee Year

We can detect this theme of solidarity in some of Pope John Paul's acts in the Jubilee Year. Certainly, his call for a remission by the wealthy countries of the debt of some of the poorer developing countries is based on human solidarity. The Holy Father means that the countries of the world are connected not only by formal agreements, but by a common humanity, and that they have a coresponsibility for each other even if they never made a point of assuming such responsibility.

But the most striking expression of solidarity in all the Jubilee acts of Pope John Paul II is surely the day of pardon that he held on the first Sunday of Lent, 2000, when he led the Church in repenting of different kinds of wrong committed by Christians in the course of the second millennium. People

have criticized the pope for this repentance by saying: Pope John Paul has not harmed any Jews; how
can he meaningfully repent of the harm inflicted by
other Christians who lived in earlier times? Such a
question is vintage individualism; such a questioner
is simply out of touch with the moral solidarity in
which Pope John Paul stands with all fellow Catholics in all earlier ages. It is true that the pope is
not coresponsible for antisemitic crimes committed
before his lifetime; such a co-responsibility does
not make any sense. But there are different kinds of
moral solidarity.

Suppose you are a parent and that a child of yours
commits some crime. Is it not perfectly meaningful
for you as parent to apologize to the family of the
victim, not as if you had some share in the guilt of
your child (perhaps your child committed the crime
in spite of everything you had taught him or her),
but simply out of the moral solidarity that one has
with one's child? It would be that extreme individualism all over again if you thought that you as parent
were in no way in the debt of the family of the victim. Well, Pope John Paul II, as head of the Catholic Church, stands in a somewhat similar kind of
moral solidarity with all Catholics, living and dead,

so that it is entirely meaningful for him to repent of wrong done by Catholics in earlier times. He does not thereby free himself (or anyone else) from any personal sin, but he "cleanses the memory" of the Church, as he puts it, and frees the Church from a collective burden of a guilt that oppresses it. And all this because of the way in which the members of the Church stand in a profound moral solidarity with each other, existing as members of each other.

WHAT IS PERSONALISM?[1]

The men and women of our time are ever more aware of themselves as persons. We experience as never before the incomparable worth of each person. We are alive to our inviolability, that is, we know in a new way that none of us is ever rightly used and destroyed for the good of others. We are more sensitive than our ancestors to all the forms of coercion that threaten our personhood. We reject the ancient distinction between Greek and barbarian; we know that the birthright of a person belongs not to a select few but to every human being. This awakening of human beings to personal existence is an epochal event, a sea-change in the way we understand ourselves.

1. This essay was originally commissioned by The Personalist Project (www.thepersonalistproject.org) and appears here with its founders' kind permission.

Now personalism is nothing other than the philosophical reflection on this new self-understanding of human beings. Personalist thinkers try to articulate it, to relate it to earlier understandings of human beings, to protect it against excess, to draw out its social consequences, and to achieve a more personalist form of religious existence.

There are different strands and schools of personalism; I am especially indebted to the Christian personalism of Karol Wojtyla (John Paul II). Wojtyla was led to think deeply about the interiority of each person and to understand that each exists as subject, not as object, or in other words, as someone, not as something, or in still other words, as self-determining, not determined. According to the personalism that he represents, a human person does not exist just to provide an instance of the human kind, but exists as this unrepeatable person and so stands in a sense above the human kind, being always more than an instance of it. This personalism understands the "infinite abyss of existence" (John Henry Newman) in the interiority of each person, in virtue of which each always exceeds the finite qualities and properties that he or she displays.

Rooted in Judeo-Christian revelation

According to most personalists, this sense of personal existence has emerged in the encounter with the living God of Judeo-Christian revelation. It can be sustained and deepened only if we continue to live in this encounter. Those who repudiate God cannot preserve the personalist affirmation of the incomparable worth of each person, though they may for a time live by the light of a setting sun. Nietzsche understood this; he understood that once God is dead, we are at liberty to acknowledge real worth only in a few human beings of exceptional quality and to contrast these with the vast run of deficient and misbegotten human beings, whom we are at liberty to scorn as having relatively little worth. Only Jews and Christians have the spiritual resources to acknowledge unconditional worth in all human persons.

Solidarity and co-responsibility

Our personalism has the effect of transforming the way we understand our social lives. We can no longer live in the social solidarity that was natural in earlier times. Parents no longer choose the profession and the spouse of their children; they acknowledge that these are choices that can only be made by their children. We can no longer share the faith of our group merely out of loyalty to the group; as persons each of us acts in his or her own name in making basic commitments of one's life. This is because persons are never mere parts in any social whole; we never exist in a social whole in the way in which organs and cells exist in a body. A human society is not a whole composed of parts, but rather, in the felicitous expression of Jacques Maritain, a whole composed of wholes.

It may seem to follow from this that personalism is just another species of individualism and is sure to bring severe social fragmentation in its wake. But most personalists have been very sensitive to the sterility of individualism. They have taken very seriously the interpersonal relations in which human persons live and move and have their being. The interiority of a person does not isolate a person from others, but rather opens him or her to others. Personalists refuse to think about social life only in terms of rights and of protection against intruders; they also think in terms of solidarity and co-responsibility. The personalism of Wojtyla aims at a solidarity that is precisely based on the fact that each member, as person, is always more than a mere part of the community, and yet at the same time that persons in community are in some way "members of each other." For personalism the ideal of a *communio personarum* (communion of persons) represents the only valid form of all deeper social life.

Incarnational personalism

Personalists divide over the question of the bodily nature of human persons. Some posit a sharp antithesis between self and body, as if a person's body were among the objects that a person deals with and as if it were just an instrument to be used for acting in the world. They see something sub-personal in the idea of a person being a bodily person. But other personalists strongly affirm just this bodily being of human persons. A person's body is not just an object for that person but it enters into his or her subjectivity. We do not just use our bodies instrumentally, but we exist as embodied. One has distinguished between dualistic personalism and incarnational personalism, and Wojtyla is emphatically incarnational.

On the other hand, the personalists inspired by him take great care not to abandon the distinction between matter and spirit in human persons; in fact they insist on the ineliminable duality of matter and spirit, and in doing so make no concession to the objectionable dualism.

The difference between the two personalist approaches to the human body gives rises to two opposed approaches to the man-woman distinction. For the dualistic personalism, that which is male or female is primarily the body, the person being neither male nor female; whereas for the incarnational personalism sexual identity is not confined to the body but informs the whole human person.

The personalism to which Wojtyla is committed sees in the incarnate condition of human persons nothing unworthy of persons; he rather discerns in it a mysterious personalization of the material world. In fact we personalists discern in it the basis for the particular place of the human person in the created world. Human persons exist on the border of matter and spirit; in them matter is spiritualized and spirit is enmattered. They have, as has been said, a kind of priestly function in creation, mediating in themselves between matter and spirit. But their mediating function is in evidence only if they are fully acknowledged as the incarnate persons that they are.

Personalist ethics

Since personalism takes seriously the freedom of persons, it takes seriously the moral existence of persons. Moral good and evil form the axis of the personal universe. The encounter with the moral law in conscience stirs the waters of personal existence like nothing else in our experience. When it comes to the norms of a personalist ethics we start with the prohibition on using persons, and proceed to condemn all the forms of coercion that do some violence to persons. In developing an ethics of respect for persons Wojtyla's personalism guards against two opposite errors. On the one hand, it rejects the ethical eudaemonism according to which the main point of the moral life is to achieve our own happiness; against this it affirms the transcendence of the moral subject who shows respect to persons because respect is due to them. On the other hand, it rejects the ethical altruism which asserts the claims of others so forcefully that any interest in our own happiness is made to appear as selfish;

against this it affirms that the moral subject is also a person and thus also one who may not simply be used, or let himself be used, for the good of others.

The personalism to which I am committed includes a particularly rich concept that has recently arisen within ethics, namely the concept of the individual moral calls addressed to particular persons. The idea is that I am not only subject to universal moral laws that bind all persons in the same way, but am also subject to particular moral calls that grow out of my unsubstitutable self and out of my encounter with other unsubstitutable selves—calls that address me and no other. If my entire moral existence consisted only in doing what any morally conscientious person would do, then I would overlook these personal calls, and my moral existence would lack its full personalist range. At the same time, personalism takes care to avoid the extreme of holding that our entire moral existence consists only in following personal calls, of holding that a personalist ethics has no use for universal moral norms, as if these were inherently de-personalizing. We are personalists who look for the unity of the unrepeatably personal and the universally human, and we do not set them against each other.

Person and consciousness

So far we have distinguished Wojtyla's personalism from individualistic personalism, from dualistic personalism, and from antinomian personalism. We have still to distinguish it from what has been called "actualistic" personalism, which says that human beings are persons just to the degree that they are consciously alive and self-present. One says this because interiority and freedom, which are so fundamental to personal being, presuppose consciousness. One infers that a human being who gives no evidence of conscious life (such as an embryo) cannot be a person. Personhood, one says, is proportioned to consciousness. But those inspired by Wojtyla's personalism hold that personhood in fact exceeds consciousness in the sense that most of us, in our conscious self-presence, fall short of the persons who we really are. The factual condition of our conscious lives does not fully manifest, and sometimes it obscures rather than manifests, the glorious birthright of existing as person. This means that our being as person far exceeds, and may even precede, our conscious self-experience.

Humans and Animals

Personalism can also go wrong in its approach to animals. It has sometimes divided the world between persons and things and has assigned all animals to things. This has the result of commodifying animals and of treating them as raw materials that exist for no other reason than to serve human need. Personalism has lost its way if it fights for the dignity of persons but at the same time thinks that animals have only instrumental value. Of course, it is quite correct to mark an essential difference between persons and non-persons, and to refuse to ascribe rights to non-personal animals. But the higher conscious animals are surely something more than mere things for our use. To treat them cruelly is wrong not only because we are more likely to treat human persons cruelly; treating them cruelly is wrong in its own right, apart from the impact of our treatment on human persons. Authentic personalism does not accept the over-simple division into persons and things; it acknowledges all kinds of beings that are less than persons but vastly more than things, and it approaches them with reverence.

34458505R00066